Sports Illustrated Kids: Legend vs. Legend

MARTA
VS.
MIA HAMM

SOCCER LEGENDS FACE OFF

by Elliott Smith

CAPSTONE PRESS
a capstone imprint

Published by Capstone Press, an imprint of Capstone
1710 Roe Crest Drive, North Mankato, Minnesota 56003
capstonepub.com

Copyright © 2026 by Capstone. All rights reserved. No part of this publication may be reproduced in whole or in part, or stored in a retrieval system, or transmitted in any form or by any means, electronic, mechanical, photocopying, recording, or otherwise, without written permission of the publisher.

SPORTS ILLUSTRATED KIDS is a trademark of ABG-SI LLC. Used with permission.

Library of Congress Cataloging-in-Publication Data
Names: Smith, Elliott, author.
Title: Marta vs. Mia Hamm : soccer legends face off / by Elliott Smith.
Other titles: Marta versus Mia Hamm
Description: North Mankato, MN : Capstone Press, [2026] | Series: Sports illustrated kids: legend vs. legend | Includes bibliographical references and index. | Audience: Ages 9-11 | Audience: Grades 4-6 | Summary: "Marta and Mia Hamm are two of the greatest soccer players ever. Marta thrilled fans from Brazil and around the world with her dazzling footwork and exciting goals. Mia Hamm used her blazing speed and amazing skills around the net to help the United States win two of the first three Women's World Cups. Which player is the all-time best? Young readers will enjoy comparing the amazing feats of these two soccer legends"— Provided by publisher.
Identifiers: LCCN 2024054352 (print) | LCCN 2024054353 (ebook) | ISBN 9798875218507 (hardcover) | ISBN 9798875218453 (paperback) | ISBN 9798875218460 (pdf) | ISBN 9798875218477 (epub) | ISBN 9798875218484 (kindle edition)
Subjects: LCSH: Vieira, Marta, 1986- —Juvenile literature. | Women soccer players—Brazil—Biography—Juvenile literature. | Hamm, Mia, 1972- —Juvenile literature. | Women soccer players—United States—Biography—Juvenile literature.
Classification: LCC GV942.7.V515 S65 2026 (print) | LCC GV942.7.V515 (ebook) | DDC 796.334092 [B]—dc23/eng/20250110
LC record available at https://lccn.loc.gov/2024054352
LC ebook record available at https://lccn.loc.gov/2024054353

Editorial Credits
Editor: Patrick Donnelly; Designer: Elyse White; Media Researcher: Jo Miller; Production Specialist: Tori Abraham

Image Credits
Associated Press: Eraldo Peres, 15, Frank Augstein, 27, Graham Hughes/The Canadian Press, 13, PAUL WHITE, 26, Vincent Yu, 7; Getty Images: Alex Grimm/Bongarts, 25, DON EMMERT/AFP, 24, John Todd/ISI Photos, 14, TIMOTHY A. CLARY/AFP, 28; Shutterstock: saicle (background), cover and throughout; Sports Illustrated: Al Tielemans, 10, 20, 22, David E. Klutho, 21, Erick W. Rasco, 5, 9, 11, 19, 29, John W. McDonough, 18, Peter Read Miller, 16, Robert Beck, cover (right), 4, 6, 8, 12, Simon Bruty, cover (left), 17, 23

Any additional websites and resources referenced in this book are not maintained, authorized, or sponsored by Capstone. All product and company names are trademarks™ or registered® trademarks of their respective holders.

Contents

Soccer Stars Face Off! 4
Physical Stats 6
Matches Played 8
Goals Scored 10
Assists 12
National Team Appearances 14
World Cup Wonders 16
World Cup Goals 18
Olympic Glory 20
Olympic Scoring 22
Hat Tricks 24
Honors and Awards 26
Who Is the Best? 28

     Glossary 30
     Read More 31
     Internet Sites 31
     Index 32
     About the Author 32

* * * Marta's stats are current through August 2024. * * *
Words in **bold** appear in the glossary.

Soccer Stars Face Off!

Mia Hamm and Marta are two of the greatest soccer players ever. They helped make women's soccer a global sport. Both have starred in big tournaments. Hamm was known for her speed. Marta has amazing footwork. But which player is the best? You decide!

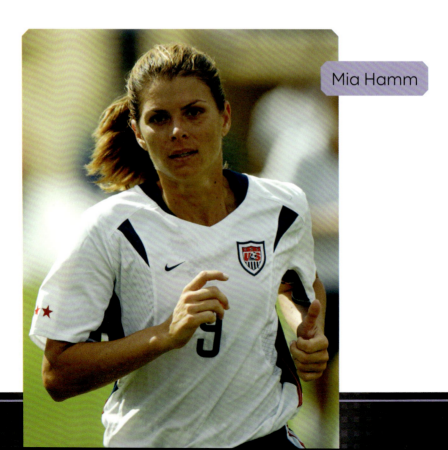

Mia Hamm

Marta

THE MATCHUP	Born	Place
Marta	February 19, 1986	Dois Riachos, Brazil
Mia Hamm	March 17, 1972	Selma, Alabama

Physical Stats

Marta and Hamm played as forwards. They have similar body types. Forwards are usually tall. That helps them battle defenders for headers. But Marta and Hamm are slightly shorter than average. Their speed and knowledge of the game helped them create scoring opportunities.

Hamm in action against Mexico in 2003

Marta takes a shot against Germany in the 2008 Olympics.

THE MATCHUP	Height	Weight
Marta	5 feet, 4 inches (163 centimeters)	128 pounds (58 kg)
Mia Hamm	5 feet, 5 inches (165 cm)	132 pounds (60 kg)

Matches Played

Marta began playing **professional** soccer at 14. She joined the Brazil women's **national team** two years later. She played 432 matches. Hamm started with the U.S. Women's National Team (USWNT) at 15. She played in the first U.S. professional women's league as part of her 329 total matches.

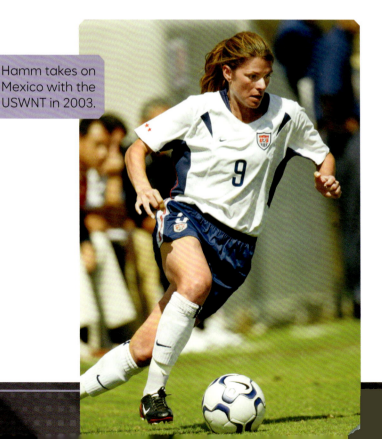

Hamm takes on Mexico with the USWNT in 2003.

Marta prepares to take a free kick for Brazil in the 2023 Women's World Cup.

THE MATCHUP	Career	Total Matches
Marta	2000–present	432
Mia Hamm	1987–2004	329

Goals Scored

Both Hamm and Marta could score from anywhere. Hamm liked to **slash** into the penalty area and shoot. Her 158 international goals rank third in the world. Marta often **dribbles** past defenders to create scoring chances. She has scored 119 international goals.

Hamm shoots against Trinidad and Tobago in 2000.

Marta fights through a crowd of Canadian defenders in 2023.

THE MATCHUP	Professional Goals	International Goals
Marta	126	119
Mia Hamm	25	158

Assists

Passing was a key part of both Marta and Hamm's game. Hamm is the USWNT all-time leader in **assists** with 147. Brazil counted on Marta to score goals. She did not have as many chances to set up her teammates. Marta did pick up five assists in six matches at the 2018 Copa América tournament. She retired with 24 assists for Brazil.

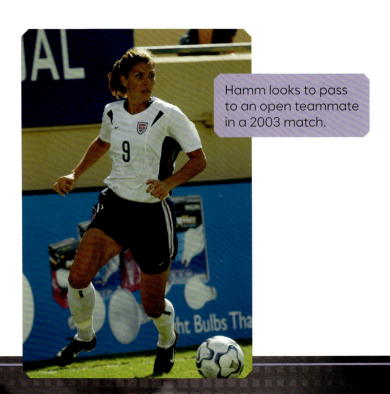

Hamm looks to pass to an open teammate in a 2003 match.

Marta dribbles past a South Korean opponent at the 2015 Women's World Cup.

THE MATCHUP	International Assists
Marta	24
Mia Hamm	147

National Team Appearances

Hamm joined the USWNT in 1987. At 15, she was the youngest ever to play on the team. She ranks fourth on the all-time list for U.S. team appearances with 276. Marta joined the Brazil national team at 16 years old. She has appeared in 185 national team matches.

Hamm celebrates after converting a penalty kick during the 1999 Women's World Cup Final against China.

Marta and USWNT defender Christie Rampone square off in a 2014 match.

THE MATCHUP	National Matches
Marta	185
Mia Hamm	276

World Cup Wonders

The World Cup is the sport's biggest stage. Hamm played in four Women's World Cups. Marta has played in six. In 2019, Marta became the first player to score in five **consecutive** World Cups. But she did not win the World Cup title. Hamm was part of the winning U.S. team in 1991 and 1999.

Hamm in action against Mexico in 1999

Marta faces U.S. opponents at the 2007 Women's World Cup.

THE MATCHUP	World Cups
Marta	6 (2003, 2007, 2011, 2015, 2019, 2023)
Mia Hamm	4 (1991, 1995, 1999, 2003)

World Cup Goals

Hamm scored her first World Cup goal in her 17th match. She finished her career with eight World Cup goals. She scored two goals in each of her four World Cup appearances. Marta has a record 17 World Cup goals.

Hamm charges toward the net in a 1999 Women's World Cup match against China.

Marta blasts a shot against Australia during the 2023 Women's World Cup.

THE MATCHUP	World Cup Goals
Marta	17
Mia Hamm	8

Olympic Glory

Hamm and Marta played in the Olympics. Hamm competed in three Olympics. She won gold medals in 1996 and 2004. Marta's appearance in the 2024 Paris Games was her sixth. But the gold medal remained **elusive** for the soccer legend.

Hamm (second from left) and her teammates celebrate after receiving their 2004 Olympic gold medals.

Marta chases down a ball in a match against Great Britain at the 2012 Olympics.

THE MATCHUP	Olympic Appearances	Medals
Marta	6 (2004, 2008, 2012, 2016, 2020, 2024)	3 (silver)
Mia Hamm	3 (1996, 2000, 2004)	3 (2 gold, 1 silver)

Olympic Scoring

The Olympics brought out the best in both Marta and Hamm. Marta scored 13 Olympic goals in her six appearances. She scored three goals in the 2020 Olympics. Marta ended her Olympic career in 2024. Hamm picked up five Olympic goals in her three trips.

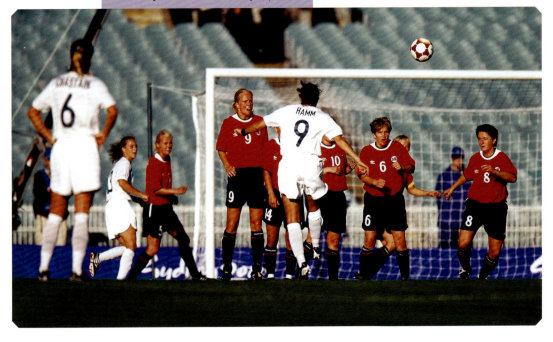

Hamm takes a free kick against Norway at the 2000 Olympics.

Marta works around a challenge by the USWNT's Kate Markgraf during the 2008 Olympics gold-medal match.

THE MATCHUP	Olympic Goals
Marta	13
Mia Hamm	5

Hat Tricks

The hat trick is one of the most amazing feats in soccer. It means one player scored three goals in the same game. Hamm holds the record for most hat tricks in international play with 10. Marta had five.

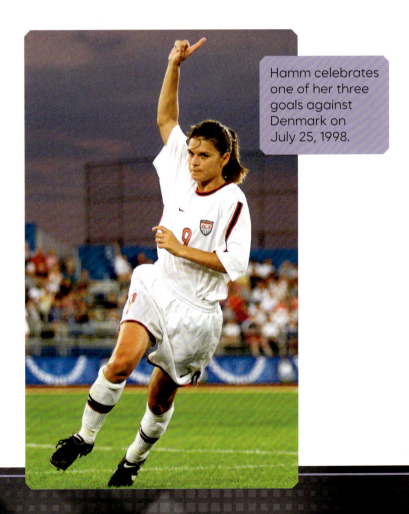

Hamm celebrates one of her three goals against Denmark on July 25, 1998.

Marta controls the ball in a 2015 match against Germany.

THE MATCHUP	Hat Tricks
Marta	5
Mia Hamm	10

Honors and Awards

Hamm was named the World Player of the Year in 2001 and 2002. She also was the first woman in the World Football Hall of Fame. Marta is a six-time World Player of the Year. She earned the Golden Ball in 2007. It is given to the best player in the World Cup.

Hamm and Brazilian striker Ronaldo receive their World Player of the Year awards in 2002.

Marta shows off her 2010 World Player of the Year award.

THE MATCHUP	Honors and Awards
Marta	World Player of the Year (six times), 2007 World Cup Golden Ball, WPS Player of the Year (twice)
Mia Hamm	World Player of the Year (twice), U.S. Soccer Female Athlete of the Year (five times), World Football Hall of Fame

Who Is the Best?

Marta and Mia Hamm are both soccer superstars. Marta's **agility** and skill give her the goal-scoring advantage. Hamm's exciting play led to Olympic and World Cup glory. Who is the best? You make the call!

Hamm celebrates after scoring against Denmark during the 1999 Women's World Cup.

Marta prepares to face Jamaica at the 2023 Women's World Cup.

Glossary

agility (uh-JILL-uh-tee)—the ability to be quick and graceful

assist (uh-SIST)—a pass that leads directly to a goal

consecutive (kun-SEK-yu-tiv)—following one after the other in order

dribble (DRIB-bul)—to move the ball downfield using one's feet

elusive (uh-LOO-suv)—hard to grasp or achieve

national team (NA-shun-uhl TEEM)—a team that represents a country

professional (pruh-FESH-uhn-uhl)—making money to do a job

slash (SLASH)—to move forward quickly with purpose

tournament (TURN-uh-munt)—a series of games between teams that help determine an overall winner

Read More

Berglund, Bruce R. *Soccer GOATs: The Greatest Athletes of All Time*. North Mankato, MN: Capstone, 2024.

Gish, Ashley. *National Women's Soccer League*. Minneapolis: Bellwether Media, 2025.

Nelson, Kristen Rajczak. *Mia Hamm: Soccer GOAT*. Buffalo, NY: Gareth Stevens Publishing, 2024.

Internet Sites

Kiddle: United States Women's National Soccer Team Facts for Kids
kids.kiddle.co/United_States_women%27s_national_soccer_team

Mia Hamm Foundation
miafoundation.org/about-mia

The Players' Tribune: Let the Girl Play
theplayerstribune.com/posts/marta-soccer-let-the-girl-play

Index

assists, 12, 13

goals scored, 10, 11, 28

Golden Ball, 26, 27

hat tricks, 24, 25

matches played, 8, 9

national team appearances, 14, 15

Olympics, 7, 20, 21, 22, 23, 28

World Cups, 9, 13, 14, 16, 17, 18, 19, 26, 27, 28, 29

World Football Hall of Fame, 26, 27

World Player of the Year, 26, 27

About the Author

Elliott Smith is a freelance writer, editor, and author. He has covered a wide variety of subjects, including sports, entertainment, and travel, for newspapers, magazines, and websites. He has written more than 70 children's books both in fiction and nonfiction. He lives in the Washington, D.C., area with his wife and two children.